WHO'S HAUNTING THE
WHITE HOUSE?

WHO'S HAUNTING THE WHITE HOUSE?

THE PRESIDENT'S MANSION AND
THE GHOSTS WHO LIVE THERE

Written by JEFF BELANGER

Illustrated by RICK POWELL

STERLING

New York / London

Library of Congress Cataloging-in-Publication Data

Belanger, Jeff.
Who's haunting the White House?: the president's mansion
and the ghosts who live there /
Jeff Belanger ; illustrated by Rick Powell.
p. cm.
Includes bibliographical references and index.
ISBN 978-1-4027-3822-7
1. White House (Washington, D.C.) 2. Ghosts--Washington (D.C.)
3. Haunted houses--Washington (D.C.) I. Powell, Rick. II. Title.
BF1472.U6B45 2008
133.1'29753--dc22
2007043375
10 9 8 7 6 5 4 3 2 1

Published by Sterling Publishing Co., Inc.
387 Park Avenue South, New York, NY 10016
Text copyright © 2008 by Jeff Belanger
Illustrations copyright © 2008 by Rick Powell
Distributed in Canada by Sterling Publishing
c/o Canadian Manda Group, 165 Dufferin Street
Toronto, Ontario, Canada M6K 3H6
Distributed in the United Kingdom by GMC Distribution Services
Castle Place, 166 High Street, Lewes, East Sussex, England BN7 1XU
Distributed in Australia by Capricorn Link (Australia) Pty. Ltd.
P.O. Box 704, Windsor, NSW 2756, Australia

Sterling ISBN 978-1-4027-3822-7

For information about custom editions, special sales, premium and
corporate purchases, please contact Sterling Special Sales Department at
800-805-5489 or specialsales@sterlingpublishing.com.

Design by Ponderosa Pine Design, Vicky Vaughn Shea

Contents

Many ghosts are said to have been seen walking the grounds just beyond the fence that protects the White House.

Welcome to the White House

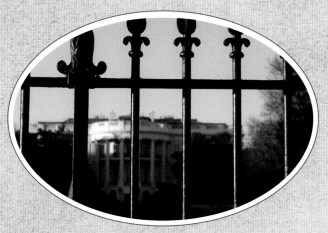

Welcome to 1600 Pennsylvania Avenue in Washington, DC, the address of a very famous and very *haunted* building better known as the White House. It's where the President of the United States lives and works while in office. This majestic building holds the President's family, pets, and a large staff of butlers, chefs, security, and other personnel. About 100 people work to keep the White House running, people who are employed by the government and have a job to do regardless of who is President. The White House has room for parties, meetings, important government events, and, according to many reports, it also has room for ghosts.

That's right, ghosts—and we're not talking about people dancing under white sheets or anything from a Halloween fun house. The White House is one of the most haunted places in the world, and we're about to explore it. But if we're going to conduct a proper ghost investigation here, we'll need to know what went into the construction and preservation of this mansion, who once lived here, and what the building means to the country. So pick up your notebook and a pen, keep your eyes wide open for darting shadows and ghostly figures, and let's start investigating.

As you walk around the outside of the White House today, you'll notice wrought iron fences surrounding the building. Policemen and soldiers patrol the grounds. Security is a lot higher than it once was. There was a time years ago when you could walk right into the Executive Residence without even having an appointment. The seventh President, Andrew Jackson, once invited the public into the White House for his inaugural reception, although that didn't turn out to be such a good idea. Not only did hundreds of people track mud all over the floor, they stole small items from the building and ripped off parts of the curtains as souvenirs.

During World War I, sheep were used to keep the lawn of the White House from growing too long.

WHO SEES GHOSTS?

The people who are most likely to have a ghostly experience are those who spend the most time in a haunted location—people who live or work there every day. These are the folks who know every inch of the building and can tell when something is off. As we go forward with our investigation, we're going to hear from past Presidents and First Ladies, as well as from people who work inside the White House every day.

You can see how well-kept the lawn is today, but it wasn't always this way. During World War I, the twenty-eighth President, Woodrow Wilson, watched sheep grazing on the grasses outside of the mansion. The sheep were being used to crop the lawn in place of the gardeners who were off fighting for the war effort.

Let's go inside. As you walk into the building, remember that almost every single President in the history of the United States stood right where you're standing.

Through our supernatural investigation, we'll see the Presidents' ghosts and hear their voices. There are many ways the dead can speak to us, if we listen closely. When you read the words of someone who died long ago, that person's thoughts, emotions, and very essence will travel through space and time right to the page.

During our ghost investigation, we're going to be looking for signs of a haunting: cold spots, spooky corners where we get a nervous feeling and the hair stands up on the back of our necks, and murmuring voices or other sounds that have no obvious living source. More important, we will hear from people who witnessed something unexplained. For part of our journey, we will explore history, because you can't know the ghosts until you know where they came from and why.

If you're ready to begin our quest for spooks and specters, take a deep breath and let's go back to the very beginning of the United States of America.

How Did It All Begin?

It was here in Philadelphia, Pennsylvania, that the founding fathers declared their independence from England in 1776.

Let's travel back over 200 years. The place is Philadelphia, Pennsylvania, and the year is 1776. If you look around, you'll see no cars, no airplanes, no streetlights, and although there's no electricity, there's certainly something electric in the air. A nation is about to be born.

On July 4, 1776, the United States declared its independence from England. The country still celebrates July 4th every year with picnics, parades, and firework displays. Back in 1776 there were explosions, too, but these explosions were from battles fought during what came to be known as the Revolutionary War. More than 25,000 Americans died in the bloody conflict between the United States and England. Some soldiers lost their lives on the battlefield, others in prison, and some from diseases related to injuries received in the war.

Certainly many a ghost still haunts the battlefields where these brave people made their last stand. We should make a note of this for a future ghost investigation, but for now let's return to the White House.

When the Revolutionary War ended in 1781, the United States was free to run itself, to write its own Constitution, and to build a formal government. This was no easy task, and there were many arguments at the 1787 Constitutional Convention about how things should work. But one issue that the founders of the United States did agree on was that the nation needed a capital and its leader needed a place to sleep.

In March of 1792, Founding Father Thomas Jefferson ran a contest encouraging architects to submit their ideas on what the presidential palace should look like. The prize was $500 or a medal, and the submissions were judged by George Washington himself. Many designs came in, but none excited General Washington, so he went in search of the right person to do the job.

President Washington recalled hearing about a gifted designer and builder in Charleston, South Carolina, an Irish architect named James Hoban. Hoban went to Philadelphia to meet with

George Washington at the first President's request. The two discussed their ideas about what the mansion should look like. The President thought it should be similar in design to his own mansion in Mount Vernon, Virginia, and James Hoban complied with the request. Not surprisingly, Mr. Hoban's submission won the contest.

Hoban designed the plans for the White House in a style called Georgian, named after King George III of England, the very king the United States had just fought against in a bloody war of independence.

George Washington chose a location for the White House in the center of the District of Columbia. (The District of Columbia was the original name of the United States's capital city, Washington, DC.) There President Washington oversaw the laying of the building's first cornerstone in a ceremony that took place in October of 1792. The President's mansion, which took eight years to complete, was built by slaves on loan from local plantations and over 100 skilled workers, who knew how to work with stone, cement, and wood. By October of 1800, the mansion was complete enough for the President to move in. But President Washington never spent a single night in the White House.

The winning White House design went to James Hoban, who created a plan for the building that was similar to President George Washington's house in Mount Vernon, Virginia.

In 1792, Thomas Jefferson ran this ad, advertising a prize of $500 to the person with the best design for the White House.

He died on December 14, 1799, less than one year before the mansion was completed.

The land on which the White House sits was donated by David Burns in 1790. This is an important name to remember because it seems that Mr. Burns may still be around all these years later. In 1961, Lillian Rogers Parks, a seamstress in the White House for 30 years, wrote about her experiences in the famous haunted house. Ms. Parks recalled being told by Cesar Carrera, a valet to President Franklin Delano Roosevelt, that "he had heard someone calling him in a strange, far-off voice in the Yellow Room, and telling him that his

WASHINGTON, in the Territory of COLUMBIA.

A PREMIUM

OF FIVE HUNDRED DOLLARS, or a MEDAL of that value, at the option of the party, will be given by the Commissioners of the Federal Buildings, to the person who, before the fifteenth day of July next, shall produce to them the most approved PLAN, if adopted by them, for a PRESIDENT's HOUSE, to be erected in this City. The fite of the building, if the artist will attend to it, will of course influence the aspect and outline of his plan; and it's destination will point out to him the number, size, and distribution of the apartments. It will be a recommendation of any plan, if the central part of it may be detached and erected for the present, with the appearance of a complete whole, and be capable of admitting the additional parts, in future, if they shall be wanting. Drawings will be expected of the ground plats, elevations of each front, and sections through the building, in such directions as may be necessary to explain the internal structure; and an estimate of the cubic feet of brick-work composing the whole mass of the walls.

March 14, 1792.   tf   THE COMMISSIONERS.

This is how the White House looked for its first few Presidents. No ghosts here in 1817 . . . not just yet.

name was 'Mr. Burns.'" But when Carrera reached the entrance of the room, he found that no one was there. He didn't learn until later that Mr. Burns was the original landowner.

A few years after Cesar Carrera heard the strange voice, a security guard who was working in the White House during President Truman's term heard a voice call, "I'm Mr. Burns" from upstairs. The guard assumed this was President Truman's Secretary of State, James Byrnes (spelled differently, but pronounced the same). But the guard found no one upstairs and later learned that Secretary Byrnes wasn't even at the White House that day. There is certainly something about 1600 Pennsylvania Avenue that keeps people here. We've just found a ghost who dates back to before the cornerstone of the building was even laid.

Moving In

On November 1, 1800, John Adams became the first person to spend the night in the White House. But this majestic building wasn't called the White House back then. Some referred to the building as the "President's Palace," or the "Executive Mansion." The name "White House" wouldn't come until a century later when the twenty-sixth President, Theodore Roosevelt, gave the building that moniker.

When John Adams, the second President of the United States, arrived at the White House, there was hardly any furniture in the Executive Residence, some of the plaster walls were still wet, and parts of the mansion still needed to be completed. Adams no doubt walked into his new home and felt the chilly drafts coming through the unfinished walls, and he saw tools and building materials lying in piles on the floor.

When Abigail Adams moved in later that same month, the building had 64 rooms on three levels, but not all of the rooms were finished yet. The Adamses had to live among workers who were putting the finishing touches on various walls and completing the main staircase.

The outside walls of the President's house are four feet thick—built to withstand a cannonball—but at first, the mansion was not a very comfortable home for John and Abigail Adams. Its fireplaces offered the only relief from chilly autumns and winters, but the rooms were so large that unless you could get close to the fire, you still needed a coat! There was very little furniture or decoration back then. Because the rooms were so empty, each footstep echoed off the marble floors and the twenty-foot-high ceilings.

When First Lady Abigail Adams moved into 1600 Pennsylvania Avenue, there was practically no furniture, and comforts were few.

Although Abigail Adams had to give up many of the comforts she was accustomed to at her home in Braintree, Massachusetts, to live in the stark and drafty Executive Mansion, she made the most of the space, using the White House's East Room as a place to hang her laundry. It seems she is still doing so. Many people have reported an almost transparent woman hanging ghostly laundry in the East Room long after the Adamses moved out and died. Witnesses stare for a moment and then the vision vanishes. Other people have reported the smell of soap and wet laundry in addition to seeing a vision of Abigail Adams. Although she lived there for only one year, Abigail Adams is thought to be among the many ghosts still inhabiting the White House.

From here, our ghost investigation will take us a dozen years into the future, to 1814 and America's next war, and to the White House's darkest days. After all, where there are wars, there are ghosts.

THE DEAD SPEAK . . .

On November 2, 1800, President Adams wrote this letter to his wife, Abigail, who was still at their home in Massachusetts:

My dearest friend.
We arrived here last night, or rather yesterday, at one o'clock and here we dined and slept. The building is in a state to be habitable. And now we wish for your company . . . Before I end my letter I pray Heaven to bestow the best of blessings on this house and all that shall hereafter inhabit it. May none but honest and wise men ever rule under this roof. . . . [1]

The East Room of the White House looks very different today compared to when Abigail Adams lived here.

Some witnesses claim to have seen the ghost of Mrs. Adams hanging her laundry in this large room.

Tragedy Strikes the White House

James Madison, the fourth President of the United States.

The White House was still a very young building when tragedy first struck. The year was 1814 and America was at war again. Like many ghost investigations, this one will be grim work as we're forced to explore and sometimes relive some of history's darkest moments.

In January of 1809, James Madison became the fourth President of the United States. He and his wife, Dolley, moved into the White House in early March of that year, and by the end of his first term in office, President James Madison had a war brewing in his country.

First Lady Dolley Madison narrowly escaped the White House with her life when the British army attacked Washington, DC, in 1814.

On August 24, 1814, the Executive Mansion and many other buildings in Washington were burned to the ground by the British.

The War of 1812 was also known as the second American Revolution because the Americans were once again fighting the British. The British were boarding American sailing ships headed for what England considered enemy countries, and seizing the ship's cargo. This wasn't taken very well by the Americans, and tensions rose between the two countries until war was declared on June 18, 1812.

The War of 1812 came roaring into Washington, DC, and right to President and Mrs. Madison's door in August of 1814.

WHY GHOSTS?

When bad things happen in and around a building, ghosts will often appear. Why this happens, we can only guess. Some theories are that these ghosts died very quickly and don't even realize that they're dead. They just wander around looking for their friends or family. Or perhaps their sense of duty keeps them bound to a location forever. Every now and again, one of these specters is spotted by the living, and that can be a very frightening experience.

Another theory is that these spirits have unfinished business—something they feel they must do before they can move on. A ghost may simply be an impression of something that happened in the area long ago. The scene just plays over and over like a movie, and sometimes we catch a glimpse of that movie. No matter the reason, ghosts are all around us, and we find them most often where there have been catastrophes, battles, destruction, and loss of life.

(It's certainly strange to call a war "The War of 1812" when it was still being fought in 1814, but they named this war after the year it began.) Fifty British ships and 4,000 soldiers landed just outside of Washington, DC, and marched toward the capital.

Mrs. Madison and her staff of servants spent Wednesday, August 24, 1814, preparing a large dinner for the president's cabinet and several military personnel. The dining table was set, but the dinner wasn't to be eaten by any Americans. By late afternoon, the White House staff had to flee or face capture by the British. Meanwhile, British soldiers stormed through Washington, DC, burning not only the buildings that were considered military targets, but setting fire to every public building, including the White House. The soldiers stopped only long enough to eat the dinner prepared by Mrs. Madison and her staff.

When the British soldiers left, the mighty mansion was in ruin. Just short of the building's fourteenth birthday, it was nothing more than a smoldering shell. Everything inside was burned to ashes, and the thick, white walls of stone stood cracked and battered from the intense heat of the fire. The city of Washington, DC, was almost completely destroyed.

The British troops had hoped that this act would drive a lethal blow to the new nation, but that was not the case. Too many had fought too hard and given too much in the American Revolution so the United States could be a free country. Within days, the American military regrouped and the British army was driven back to its boats, waiting in nearby Chesapeake Bay.

THE DEAD SPEAK . . .

On Tuesday, August 23, 1814, Mrs. Madison began writing a letter to her sister detailing the situation around her in Washington.

Dear Sister,

My husband left me yesterday morning to join General Winder. He enquired anxiously whether I had courage, or firmness to remain in the President's house until his return, on the morrow, or succeeding day, and on my assurance that I had no fear but for him and the success of our army, he left me, beseeching me to take care of myself, and of the cabinet papers, public and private. I have since received two dispatches from him, written with a pencil; the last is alarming, because he desires I should be ready at a moment's warning to enter my carriage and leave the city; that the enemy seemed stronger than had been reported, and that it might happen that they would reach the city, with intention to destroy it . . . I am accordingly ready. . . . Wednesday morning, twelve o'clock. Since sunrise I have been turning my spyglass in every direction and watching with unwearied anxiety, hoping to discern the approach of my dear husband and his friends, but, alas, I can descry only groups of military wandering in all directions, as if there was a lack of arms, or of spirit to fight for their own firesides! Three o'clock. Will you believe it, my Sister? We have had a battle or skirmish near Bladensburg, and I am still here within sound of the cannon! Mr. Madison comes not; may God protect him! Two messengers covered with dust, come to bid me fly. . . . Dear sister, I must leave this house, or the retreating army will make me a prisoner in it, by filling up the road I am directed to take. When I shall again write you, or where I shall be tomorrow, I cannot tell! [2]

During the raid on Washington, the British fought and burned their way through the city. In the background, the White House is engulfed in flames.

After the battle that left the White House and much of the city of Washington, DC, in ashes, there were some who wanted to move the capital far away from the coast. There, they believed, the city would be safer from attack. But President Madison wouldn't hear of it. He wanted everything rebuilt exactly where it stood as a signal to England, and to any other country that tried to invade, that the United States would not back down and would not be defeated.

The White House was going to be rebuilt, and once again architect James Hoban was hired for the job. Many reports of the day called the task a "minor repair," but this was a bit of political spin so that people in the United States would continue to have confidence that their government in Washington was still fully operational. The reality was that Hoban and his crew were basically starting over with the White House. Only the outer walls could be salvaged in the rebuilding. When Hoban rebuilt, he also added two new distinguishing features to the President's mansion—a North and South Portico. A portico is a roofed space, supported by columns, that usually is used as a porch. Today the North Portico is visible on the back of a $20 bill.

Take a look at today's White House. Notice how white and clean the building looks from the outside? It's been that way since it was rebuilt. Did you know it takes 570 gallons of paint to cover this building? But there are two special spots where they never paint. Just to the right of the front door and underneath the window is an unpainted spot that shows burn marks from over two hundred years ago. On the south side of the White House, near

After the War of 1812, Washington, DC, was a smoldering ruin. The White House was an empty, burned-out shell.

WHAT IS FOLKLORE?

Traditional stories, beliefs, and myths that have been passed on by word of mouth are called folklore. Folklore is a very important part of a ghost investigation because often when people see a ghost, they don't write down every detail of the experience. But they do tell others—their friends and family. Those people then pass on the incredible stories. When folklore gets passed around for many years, it can be difficult to find the source, but it's important to know that folklore always has some basis in fact. You will find that some part of the story is true, if you can just look back far enough. As a ghost investigator, it's your job to do the digging.

It takes 570 gallons of white paint to cover the White House.

But there are two spots on the building that are never painted.

The burn marks from 1814 remain so we never forget what happened.

the second-floor balcony—also called the Truman balcony—is another spot of blackened burn marks. These spots are left unpainted to remind us of what happened here back in 1814.

There is another reminder of the War of 1812. There is a story at the White House about the ghost of a British Redcoat soldier who wanders the grounds outside the mansion, near the North Portico. Some people report that he's carrying a torch, while others say it is a lantern. Because of the battle that took place in Washington, DC, there is actual history to support this ghost story. Could this soldier be one of the men who walked through Washington setting fire to the buildings, who was then shot and killed by an American's musket ball? Was he killed so fast that he didn't realize he was dead? If so, the poor man may still be searching for his fellow soldiers and carrying the ghostly torch as he looks for his ship to take him home to England.

The legend of the British ghost has been passed around for many decades, but until we can find a living person who claims to have seen the British soldier's ghost, this bit of information will have to remain folklore.

Andrew Jackson, seventh
President of the United States.

William Henry Harrison only served as
President for one month. He died
of pneumonia on April 4, 1841.

Andrew Jackson Is Angry...
William Henry Harrison Was Searching...

L et's move forward in time a bit to Andrew Jackson, the seventh President of the United States. Jackson was considered by many to be the common man's President. He was raised in the backwoods of South Carolina and wouldn't think twice about starting a brawl if his honor was at stake. In fact, Andrew Jackson once challenged a man named Charles Dickinson to a duel because Dickinson made some jokes about Jackson's wife, Rachel Donelson. Charles Dickinson chose to fight with pistols and the two men faced each other and drew their weapons. Dickinson drew first and put a bullet into Andrew Jackson's chest that broke two ribs and stopped mere inches from his heart. But the rules of the duel said that Dickinson had to stand still while Jackson returned fire. Andrew Jackson's shot was perfect and killed Dickinson almost instantly.

Andrew Jackson wasn't afraid of facing an oncoming bullet, and he never turned away from a fight. During the War of 1812, he served as a general in the army. There he earned the nickname "Old Hickory" because of how tough and rigid a leader he was when he defeated the British in the Battle of New Orleans.

When Jackson was elected President in 1829, he was considered one of the most popular presidents since George Washington. President Jackson had ideas on how simply the government could run, but this was a threatening idea to lifelong politicians who led comfortable lives by doing very little in various offices around Washington. Jackson had no patience when it came to other branches of government telling him what he could and couldn't do. In January of 1832, President Jackson was eating dinner with some friends at the White House when an assistant came over and whispered in the President's ear that the Senate had rejected his nomination of Martin Van Buren as Minister to England. The President jumped to his feet and yelled, "By the Eternal! I'll smash them!" President Jackson's friend Martin Van Buren went on to become Vice President and then President.

Although President Jackson died in 1845 at his home near Nashville, Tennessee, he may still be angry about something. During Abraham Lincoln's presidency, Lincoln's wife, Mary Todd, claimed that she heard Andrew Jackson in what was then called the Rose Guest Room in the First Family's upstairs living quarters. She claimed President Jackson's ghost was cursing and swearing as he made a ruckus in the room. President Jackson is also said to be heard laughing in the Red Room on the main floor of the White House.

"Old Hickory," his troops called him; Andrew Jackson led the American army in defeating the British in New Orleans.

Is the laughter of President Andrew Jackson still echoing in the White House's Red Room?

The Red Room was once the former President's bedroom. "Old Hickory" was certainly known for his temper in life, and it seems that it may have followed him into death.

The ninth President of the United States certainly served for the shortest period of time. While giving his one-hour-and-forty-minute inaugural address (the longest inaugural address in the history of the United States even to this day), President William Henry Harrison refused to wear a hat or coat, even though it was bitterly cold outside. Shortly after, the President caught a cold that developed into pneumonia. On April 4, 1841, one month after taking the oath of office, Harrison died in the White House, becoming the first President to die while in office.

A few years after his death, members of the White House staff reported hearing strange noises in the attic of the building. At first they thought a rodent or other animal had gotten loose up there, but when the noises persisted, they went up to investigate. One employee of the building claimed to see the ghost of the former President rummaging through some boxes. As he spent only one month in the building, it's difficult to guess what the former President might have been looking for. But whatever it was he was missing, perhaps President Harrison found it, because his ghost hasn't been reported since.

Though President Harrison's ghost has been quiet, many other spirits are making plenty of noise here. Our ghost investigation will now move ahead two decades to the most tragic and difficult presidency to take place under this roof.

A Little Boy's Ghost

Young Willie Lincoln was Abe's favorite son. He died in the White House in February of 1862, and his ghost appeared to his mother shortly afterward.

John Tyler was a widower when he took office as the nation's tenth President. His ghost has been seen in the Yellow Oval Room, kneeling and professing his love.

Abraham Lincoln's presidency had a dark cloud hanging over it before he ever set foot in the White House. The public knew that he wanted to end slavery in the United States. Tensions on the subject had been growing for years. The Southern states were threatening to secede, or break away, from the United States and form their own country. President Lincoln was determined not only to end the practice of slavery, but to keep the country together by any means necessary. He knew that a union divided would not survive.

On April 10, 1861, about a month after Lincoln became President, Brigadier General Beauregard and his Confederate forces in Charleston, South Carolina, demanded the surrender of the Union troops at Fort Sumter near the Charleston harbor. Two days later, when no word of surrender came from the fort, the Confederate forces fired their cannons and muskets at the overwhelmed and under-equipped Union soldiers inside. The Civil War had begun, and the nation was cracked in two.

Meanwhile, the Lincoln family was getting settled into their new home in the White House. The three young Lincoln sons—Robert, William, and Thomas—were animal lovers, and several Americans sent the boys gifts of dogs, rabbits, ponies, and goats to play with. The boys played games all over the building and even built a small fort on the roof of the White House.

The Lincolns loved their sons, but young Willie was the favorite. He was an especially charming, handsome, and quick-witted child. Those who encountered Willie in the White House always remembered the boy. Poet Nathaniel Parker Willis wrote about Willie Lincoln in *Home Journal* magazine:

I was one day passing the White House, when he was outside with a play-fellow on the side-walk. Mr. Seward drove in, with Prince Napoleon and two of his suite in the carriage; and, in a mock-heroic way—terms of intimacy evidently existing between the boy and the Secretary—the official gentleman took off his hat, and the Napoleon did the same, all making the young prince President a ceremonious salute. Not a bit staggered with the homage, Willie drew himself up to his full height, took off his little cap with graceful self-possession, and bowed down formally to the ground, like a little ambassador. They drove past, and he went on unconcernedly with his play: the impromptu readiness and good judgment being clearly a part of his nature. [3]

First Lady Mary Todd Lincoln wrote about seeing the ghost of her son, Willie. She even held séances–a way to communicate with the spirits of those who have died–in the White House.

Shortly after the Christmas of 1861, Willie became ill with a typhoid-type disease. His condition worsened through January and into February. His mother stayed by his bedside every day, trying to nurse Willie back to health. She dabbed his head with cool rags, read to him, and held his hand, but on February 20, 1862, after being seriously ill for two weeks, Willie passed away in his White House bedroom in the family's upstairs living quarters. The Lincolns were crushed. "It is hard, hard, hard to have him die!" President Lincoln said. Willie's funeral was held in the East Room of the White House, while his body lay in the Green Room.

President Lincoln wanted his son to be buried at home in Springfield, Illinois, but he couldn't bear to have him so far away. A friend of the President, Supreme Court Clerk William Thomas Carroll, offered Mr. Lincoln the use of his family's aboveground tomb in Oak Hill Cemetery in Washington, DC. This way, Willie Lincoln's body could be close to his family while they were in the White House. When the Lincolns moved back to Springfield, they could bring Willie home for a proper family burial. President Lincoln visited the tomb on several occasions, and even had the coffin opened so he could gaze at the face of his lost son. He wept for many hours over the loss of young Willie.

Meanwhile, tragic news of soldiers dying was coming in to the President every day. Lincoln was trying to hold the United States together by force now, and every death weighed heavily on his heart and mind. Losing his young son during all of this turmoil made this the most difficult time in the President's life. Mrs. Lincoln was also reeling. For several months after Willie's death, she stopped holding any kind of formal receptions in the Executive Mansion and refused to enter the room where her son had died.

Mary Todd Lincoln was the first to see a ghost in the White House and actually write about it. In October of 1863, she wrote to her half-sister, Emilie Todd Helm, that her son's ghost was visiting her at night:

> (H)e lives, Emilie! He comes to me every night, and stands at the foot of my bed with the same sweet, adorable smile he has always had; he does not always come alone; little Eddie [her second-born son, who died at age three] is sometimes with him, and twice he has come with our brother Alec. He tells me he loves his Uncle Alec and is with him most of the time. You cannot dream of the comfort this gives me. When I thought of my little son in immensity, alone, without his mother to direct him, no one to hold his little hand in loving guidance, it nearly broke my heart. [4]

We might want to dismiss this claim of seeing ghosts and say that Mary Todd was simply grieving for Willie and dreamed that her son had visited her. But as good ghost investigators, we need to look for other possible sightings of a young boy's ghost in the building. If we move ahead in time, we find another reference to the presence of a young boy.

INTERVIEWING THE WITNESS . . .

On July 26, 1911, Military Aide Archibald Butt wrote a letter to his sister, Clara Butt:

It seems that the White House is haunted. This was a most interesting piece of news to me, for it seemed to me to be the only thing wanting to make the White House the most interesting spot in the United States. The ghost, it seems, is a young boy from its description. . . . The housekeeper, a spooky little person herself, informs me that he has been felt more often than he has been seen, but when I remonstrated with her that ghosts have not the sense of touch, at least those self-respecting ghosts of which I have heard, she insisted that it was this manifestation of the Thing which caused such fright among the servants. [5]

Willie Lincoln wasn't the only ghost Mary Todd saw in this grand mansion. In the spring of 1862, Mrs. Lincoln was walking by the Yellow Oval Room when she heard the faint strains of a violin playing. No one was playing a musical instrument at the time, and the First Lady could not find the source of the music. She later revealed her belief that she had used some kind of psychic ability to hear Thomas Jefferson playing his violin.

Just a few days later, while walking by the Yellow Oval Room again, Mary Todd witnessed yet another unexplainable event. This time she claimed to see President John Tyler on one knee, saying, "Julia, marry me. Julia, marry me. Please be my wife!" According

to her, the former President took no notice of Mrs. Lincoln, but just continued to go through the motions of proposing.

President John Tyler died in January of 1862, just a few months before Mary Todd witnessed his presence. Perhaps Mrs. Lincoln was witnessing a replay of something that had taken place in the room just two decades earlier. After President Tyler's first wife died, the President fell in love with Julia Gardiner, a pretty woman who was 30 years younger than he. Although at first she refused to marry the President, she later reconsidered and the two became engaged in the very room where Mrs. Lincoln witnessed Tyler's proposal. Perhaps what Mary Todd Lincoln saw was not a ghost, but simply the replaying of a scene that had left an impression on the room. Some people are able to tune into a replay as if it's an old movie playing only for them. Mrs. Lincoln may have been one of those sensitive people who can see past events. But how can we tell the difference between this "psychic impression" and a real ghost? If the ghostly figure doesn't take any notice of its surroundings or the people nearby, it may just be a replaying of something that took place in that location at some point in the past. If the ghost looks at the living witness or communicates in some way, well, no old movie can do that—that's a ghost!

Now that we've determined the difference, let's press forward and examine the man who would go on to become the White House's most famous and active ghost.

MARY TODD LINCOLN'S WHITE HOUSE SÉANCES

A séance is a meeting held by someone who believes he or she can communicate with the dead. These people are called mediums, psychics, or channels. At a séance, a small group of people sit around a table. There is usually very little light during this time, perhaps just the flicker of a lone candle casting its glow on the participants.

The group holds hands as the medium begins to communicate with the ghost of a loved one.

After the death of her son Willie, Mary Todd Lincoln sought mediums who could contact Willie on her behalf. She even held some séances in the White House. President Lincoln attended one of these meetings, but this later caused problems for the President. It seems that the American people did not want to think of their President as someone who attended such gatherings. We'll never know for sure if the mediums that came to the White House really did make contact with the spirit of Willie Lincoln, but Mrs. Lincoln certainly believed they did.

President Lincoln:
Assassinated, but Not Gone

Abraham Lincoln, America's most paranormal President.

President Lincoln may have known he was doomed since his earliest days in the White House. Shortly after his election in 1860, he had an ominous vision in a mirror. When he told his wife Mary about what he saw, she believed it meant that he would not survive his second term. The President relayed this vision to Noah Brooks, a Civil War journalist, who recounted what Lincoln had said in the July 1865 issue of *Harper's New Monthly Magazine*:

It was just after my election in 1860, when the news had been coming in thick and fast all day, and there had been a great "Hurrah, boys!" so that I was well tired out, and went home to rest, throwing myself down on a lounge in my chamber. Opposite where I lay was a bureau, with a swinging glass upon it . . .

. . . and, looking in that glass, I saw myself reflected, nearly at full length; but my face, I noticed, had two separate and distinct images, the tip of the nose of one being about three inches from the tip of the other. I was a little bothered, perhaps startled, and got up and looked in the glass, but the illusion vanished. On lying down again, I saw it a second time—plainer, if possible, than before; and then I noticed that one of the faces was a little paler, say five shades, than the other. I got up and the thing melted away, and I went off and, in the excitement of the hour, forgot all about it—nearly, but not quite, for the thing would once in a while come up, and give me a little pang, as though something uncomfortable had happened. When I went home I told my wife about it, and a few days after I tried the experiment again, when [with a laugh], sure enough, the thing came again; but I never succeeded in bringing the ghost back after that, though I once tried very industriously to show it to my wife, who was worried about it somewhat. She thought it was "a sign" that I was to be elected to a second term of office, and that the paleness of one of the faces was an omen that I should not see life through the last term. [6]

President Lincoln didn't dwell on what he saw in the mirror, but he never forgot about it either. The President was occupied with running a country at war with itself, a horrible circumstance that weighed heavily on him. After his son Willie's passing, President Lincoln became more melancholy than ever. The Civil War death toll was rising. Lincoln spent many hours pacing his executive office

THE DEAD SPEAK . . .

President Lincoln told the following dream to his wife and to his friend and bodyguard, Ward Hill Lamon. Lamon retold the dream in his book *Recollections of Abraham Lincoln*, published in 1895:

About ten days ago I retired very late. I had been up waiting for important dispatches from the front. I could not have been long in bed when I fell into a slumber, for I was weary. I soon began to dream. There seemed to be a death-like stillness about me. Then I heard subdued sobs, as if a number of people were weeping. I thought I left my bed and wandered downstairs. There the silence was broken by the same pitiful sobbing, but the mourners were invisible. I went from room to room; no living person was in sight, but the same mournful sounds of distress met me as I passed along. I saw light in all the rooms; every object was familiar to me; but where were all the people who were grieving as if their hearts would break? I was puzzled and alarmed. What could be the meaning of all this? Determined to find the cause of a state of things so mysterious and so shocking, I kept on until I arrived at the East Room, which I entered. There I met with a sickening surprise. Before me was a catafalque, on which rested a corpse wrapped in funeral vestments. Around it were stationed soldiers who were acting as guards; and there was a throng of people, [some] gazing mournfully upon the corpse, whose face was covered, others weeping pitifully. "Who is dead in the White House?" I demanded of one of the soldiers. "The President," was his answer; "he was killed by an assassin!" Then came a loud burst of grief from the crowd. [1]

with his head hanging down and his hands folded behind his back, trying to think of a way to end the war and violence as quickly as possible while still holding the United States together.

By the time the next presidential election came around in 1864, many were growing weary of the war, and Lincoln's chances for reelection seemed doubtful. But a major Union victory by General Sherman in Atlanta, Georgia, gave the North hope that the end of the Civil War was near, and the country regained faith in their President. Lincoln was reelected in November of 1864.

President Lincoln's vision in the mirror wasn't the only prediction he had concerning his own death. He had another revelation in a dream shortly before that fateful day in April of 1865 when an assassin's bullet found its mark.

On the evening of April 14, 1865, Abraham Lincoln and Mary Todd headed to Ford's Theatre in Washington DC to see a play called *Our American Cousin*. Lincoln's outlook on the future of the United States was bright for the first time in years. Only a few days earlier, General Lee's Southern forces had surrendered to General Grant at the Appomattox Court House in Virginia. The end of the Civil War was here, and it was a time to celebrate and to heal the nation.

On this particular day, the President's evening bodyguard, John Parker, was running three hours late. The President told his daytime bodyguard, William Crook, that he could go home and that Mr. Parker would meet him at Ford's Theatre. William Crook protested because he didn't want to leave the President without protection, but when Lincoln insisted, Crook agreed. "Good

On April 14, 1865, John Wilkes Booth slipped unnoticed into President Lincoln's private box at Ford's Theatre and shot the President in the back of the head.

Though enemies of President Lincoln believed John Wilkes Booth was a hero, the United States government wanted to arrest and punish the people responsible for the President's assassination and was willing to pay a large reward to make that happen.

night, Mr. President," Crook said. "Good-bye, Crook," was President Lincoln's response. According to William Crook, the President always said "Good night, Crook." This was the first and only time Mr. Lincoln said "good-bye." Perhaps the President had an idea of what was to come.

The President and First Lady arrived at Ford's Theatre at 8:30 p.m. and took their seats in the State Box—the elevated private section to the side of the stage reserved for distinguished guests. What the Lincolns didn't know was that a man named John Wilkes Booth also knew that the President was going to be at the play that evening.

Shortly after 10:00 p.m., Booth entered the front of Ford's Theatre with a pistol tucked in his coat. The audience's attention was focused on the stage and not the stairway to the State Box, where Booth was creeping up the stairs toward the unsuspecting President. At 10:15, Booth quietly opened the door to the State Box, put his pistol within inches of the back of President Lincoln's head, and pulled the trigger. An audience of over 1,000 people watched in horror as the President slumped over in his seat. As Mrs. Lincoln screamed, the assassin slipped away into the night, where his horse was waiting to take him to a hideout in Maryland.

President Lincoln was carried to the Petersen House across the street from Ford's Theatre for medical attention. He survived the night, but his wound was too severe and he passed away the following morning.

President Lincoln's ghost will be the most intense part of our investigation. His figure has been spotted in various parts of the

White House, but he's seen most often in the Lincoln Bedroom. The name of this room is a little misleading because it was never actually President Lincoln's bedroom. It was the executive office of the President until the addition of the West Wing to the White House in 1902; however, the furniture once belonged to the Lincoln family. Today, distinguished guests of the current President often spend the night in the Lincoln Bedroom. This room is also one of the most actively haunted rooms in the building.

As you walk into the room, you'll notice the rosewood furniture. The bed and the bureaus are made of the expensive, red-colored wood. Mrs. Lincoln bought the furniture while she was living in the White House. Walk around. Can you feel the sense of history? Can you feel President Lincoln's presence? Can you imagine him pacing this room, worried about the Civil War?

First Lady Grace Coolidge, the wife of President Calvin Coolidge, lived in the White House from 1923 to 1929. She is said to be the first person who actually saw the ghost of Abraham Lincoln. According to Mrs. Coolidge, he was standing at a window in the Yellow Oval Room with his hands clasped behind his back, looking out over the Potomac River.

For further evidence of a haunting, we'll need to hear from witnesses. Those witnesses aren't always human. Animals have long been thought to be more sensitive to ghosts and spirits. Many times a dog or cat will act strangely in the presence of a ghost. The fortieth President, Ronald Reagan, had this to say about his pet and the Lincoln Bedroom: "Every once in a while our little dog Rex will start down that long hall toward that room, just glaring

TRYING TO CONTACT HER DEAD HUSBAND

After President Lincoln was assassinated on April 14, 1865, his widow was more distraught than ever. She had little money (back then there were no life insurance policies for the widow of the President) and few friends. Mary Todd Lincoln made her way up to Boston to seek out the services of a spirit photographer named William Mumler. The average cost for a portrait photograph at this time was fifty cents. Mumler charged ten dollars for a spirit portrait, and he guaranteed results. Mrs. Lincoln took a seat in Mumler's studio and sat very still while the photographer used a camera called a daguerreotype to take her picture. When Mumler later showed the picture to Mrs. Lincoln, she could see the ghostly figure of a tall, bearded man standing behind her.

William Mumler of Boston promised Mary Todd Lincoln that he could take a picture of her husband's spirit for $10.

William Mumler was later revealed to be a fraud. His business was investigated and it was found that some of the "ghosts" in his photographs were actually local Boston actors who were all very much alive.

GHOSTS OF ANIMALS?

Throughout history, people have reported seeing the ghosts of dogs, cats, horses, and many other animals. The White House also has its resident animal ghost. There's a White House legend that says the ghost of a black cat is spotted in the basement of the building just before times of national tragedies like the assassination of a President or the crash of the stock market.

as if he's seeing something, and barking, and he stops in front of Lincoln's door, the bedroom door." [8]

President Reagan's daughter, Maureen, was sleeping in the Lincoln Bedroom with her husband during the 1980s when she woke up and saw "an aura, sometimes red, sometimes orange." [9] Dennis Freemyer, White House Deputy Chief Usher, also had an odd experience in the Lincoln Bedroom in the 1980s. Mr. Freemyer says:

I've been here almost 25 years. I've only had one experience upstairs, and it was back during the Reagan administration. Normally we have a gentleman that works here in the evenings that turns out all the lights at the First Family's request and kind of shuts the place down for the night, but he was out sick that night so I was doing his job. And I'd gone upstairs and turned out

Mourners visit the body of President Abraham Lincoln at his official state funeral in New York.

lights in a number of rooms. I went to the Lincoln Bedroom, and there's a chandelier there that had a light switch that was a dimmer type that you just push in and it turns it off—a rheostat. So I turned that light off, turned out some other lights, went in to a series of other rooms, went across the hallway into what's called the Queen's Bedroom, and as I came out of the Queen's Bedroom, I was looking directly into a darkened Lincoln Bedroom, and all of a sudden the chandelier came back on.

Sir Winston Churchill was the prime minister of England during World War II. He may have had a rather ghost-filled night in the Lincoln Bedroom.

Of course I'd been aware of some of the stories and all, so I ran in right away, hoping that I'd get to see something or feel something and really didn't see anything at first. I turned off the chandelier, and then I got a very cold chill. I could definitely feel something, so I kind of looked around. I looked in the mirror, thinking maybe there was something behind me, which of course there wasn't. But without a doubt, I could feel a very cold presence of someone/something there.[10]

As we look back through history, we learn that there were others who had strange feelings about the Lincoln Bedroom, too. Sir Winston Churchill, the prime minister of England and also his country's minister of defense during World War II, stayed in the White House for several weeks to meet with President Roosevelt. While staying in the Executive Mansion, Prime Minister Churchill was offered the Lincoln Bedroom—one of the finest and most historically significant guest rooms in the house. Some reports say that the prime minister was very uncomfortable in the room and felt it was haunted. He spent one night there and then moved to a different guest room for the rest of his stay.

There is another bit of folklore here concerning Queen Juliana of the Netherlands, a distinguished guest of the White House during the Truman administration. In April of 1952, Queen Juliana and her husband, Prince Bernhard, stayed in the Lincoln Bedroom.

INTERVIEWING THE WITNESS...

On December 27, 1968, First Lady Claudia "Lady Bird" Johnson, the wife of the thirty-sixth President, Lyndon B. Johnson, gave an interview in which she talked about how spooky the White House can be:

I often walk around [the White House], just to sense it and drink it in. . . . There is sometimes a sense of presence. I remember one night in February, I think it was, the centennial of Lincoln's death, I was watching a very good TV drama alone in my bedroom and the fire was flickering and I looked above the mantle and my eyes came to light on the plaque that said, 'In this room Abraham Lincoln slept in the years of his Presidency 1861 to 1865.' And I get that eerie chill.[11]

There have been reports that the queen was awoken by a knock at the door in the night. When she opened the door, wearing only her bedclothes and nightgown, she saw President Lincoln's ghost standing there, which no doubt gave her quite a scare.

Tony Savoy, White House operations foreman, says he also came face-to-face with President Lincoln just outside of his former office:

It was early one morning, and I was taking care of the plants up on the second floor. I used to come in early in the morning and turn the lights on and walk down the hall in the dark. When I turned the light on one morning, he was sitting there outside his office with his hands over top of each other, legs crossed, and was looking straight ahead. He had a gray, charcoal [colored] pin-striped suit on, and he had a pair of three-button

spats turned over on the side with black shoes on. He was sitting there, and he startled me and I stopped. And when I blinked, he was gone. And I left there and went down the stairs and told Assistant Usher Nelson Pierce what I had seen. And he said I'm just one of the other ones that had seen him throughout the house over the past years.[12]

Today when you ask the Secret Service agents and the staff of the White House who is haunting this historic building, President Lincoln's name is the one that comes up most often. Given the many credible witnesses we've heard from, we must call the Lincoln Bedroom the White House's most haunted and most active room. But let's move along—there is more to investigate here.

Queen Juliana was a White House guest of President Harry Truman in April of 1952. Some have claimed that the queen saw the ghost of Abraham Lincoln during her stay.

Dolley Madison's Ghost Is Upset

Some people think that ghosts only come out at night—that the wandering spirits remain hidden during the day, unable to frighten anyone. Others believe that ghosts can only be found inside buildings—in creepy, dark attics or musty, damp basements. In 1913, some groundskeepers working at the White House learned that both of these ideas are simply not true when they saw a ghost in the gardens of the White House.

On March 4, 1913, Woodrow Wilson stood at the podium on the steps of the Capitol building in Washington, DC, and became the twenty-eighth President of the United States. After the parades and ceremonies had ended, President Wilson and his wife, First Lady Ellen Louise Wilson, had the task of moving into the White House. The Wilsons were focused on transporting their clothes, knickknacks, family photos, and other personal belongings from their home in New Jersey, so they

First Lady Ellen Louise Wilson wanted to make a few changes to the White House gardens to make her feel more at home. She didn't realize that this might stir up a ghost!

probably weren't too concerned about moving into a haunted mansion. But maybe they had heard a few accounts of a little boy's ghost wandering the halls. Maybe they found themselves looking over their shoulders to see if those footsteps belonged to a living person or not.

Shortly after moving in, the Wilsons began adding their own touches to the White House, as many First Families do. They wanted to make the mansion feel more like home, but they also wanted to leave some kind of historical mark on the property. Early in the spring of 1913, the First Lady ordered the colonial garden on the western side of the White House to be removed to make room for a lush collection of roses. She loved the look and smell of the thorny bushes.

The White House gardeners approached the western side of the building with shovels and picks, ready to carry out the wishes of the First Lady, but they froze before they could remove even one

The Colonial Garden at the White House was the location of one angry ghost back in 1913.

shovelful of dirt. Hovering above the garden was the figure of a ghostly woman. Her curly black hair surrounded a pale round face bearing a scowl of anger. Some reports said the specter had her hands on her hips, while other stories said she raised an almost see-through finger and wagged it at the workers, but all accounts agree that this woman's spirit was angry…very angry. The gardeners dropped their tools and ran off. Mrs. Wilson's garden of roses would have to wait for another day.

The groundskeepers later learned that the figure with curly black hair and a disapproving face was former First Lady Dolley Madison, who had planted the colonial garden in 1809. Mrs. Madison had adored the White House grounds and gardens and apparently did not want them disturbed in any way. Dolley had died back in 1849—sixty-four years before First Lady Ellen Louise Wilson ordered the beloved flowers to be removed—but it seems that Dolley Madison still took a great deal of pride in her garden! Sometimes spirits don't like to see their homes changed around too much, and they may let us know this in rather frightening ways.

"The Place Is Haunted, Sure as Shootin'"

President Harry S. Truman was sure the White House was haunted. He mentioned the ghosts several times in his letters.

As we investigate more modern times, we'll find that ghost reports at the White House actually seem to be increasing. More ghosts were reported in the White House during the second half of the twentieth century than ever before. There could be several reasons for this. There have been many developments in the way we chronicle events in the last hundred years. With the help of portable audio and video recording equipment, everything the Presidents say and do is now documented. If a president mentions a ghost in passing, someone will hear about it and write it down. It could also be that our culture is coming to accept the idea of ghosts. It's easy not to believe in ghosts if you've never seen one; it's almost impossible *not* to believe in ghosts if you *have*.

June 17, 1945

THE WHITE HOUSE
WASHINGTON

Dear Bess: Just two months ago today, I was a reasonably happy and contented Vice-President. Maybe you can remember that far back too. But things have changed so much it hardly seems real.

I sit here in this old house and work on foreign affairs, read reports, and work on speeches—all the while listening to the ghosts walk up and down the hall way and even right in here in the study. The floors pop and the drapes move back and forth—I can just imagine old Andy and Teddy having an argument over Franklin. Or James Buchanan and

In a letter to his wife, President Truman mentioned
the ghosts walking around the halls of the White House.

Harry S. Truman, the thirty-third President of the United States, spoke often about the ghosts in the White House. Truman briefly served as Vice President to Franklin D. Roosevelt (from January to April 1945, when Roosevelt died), and after Roosevelt's death Truman became President. He was in and around the White House during a very difficult time in America's history, which included the end of World War II.

It's been said around the White House that when the United States is at war or going through a period of great suffering, it seems to stir up the ghost of President Abraham Lincoln. Perhaps this is true, because President Truman reported quite a bit of ghostly activity in his diary, letters, and discussions with family and friends.

By the time of Truman's presidency, the White House was beginning to fall apart. A number of additions had been made from the late 1800s to the first half of the 1900s, and more servants and staff were using the building than ever before. The weight was becoming greater than the White House's wooden beams could bear. In 1948, President Truman watched as the floor sagged where large men walked, walls cracked, and plaster fell from the ceilings that were crumbling from the inside.

The President and his family moved and the White House was completely gutted and rebuilt from the inside. The mansion grew to 132 rooms. The main house was used for entertaining, formal meetings, and living quarters, and the East and West wings were used for offices.

In 1948, the White House was in danger of collapsing, so President Truman and his family moved out while the entire building was rebuilt. Though the old boards and pipes were removed, the ghosts, it seems, remain.

INTERVIEWING THE WITNESS . . .

Truman heard rumors about the White House being haunted early in his presidency. In a letter of June 30, 1947 to his wife, Bess, President Truman noted:

The ghosts walked and walked last night. I left all the doors open. That gave me a chance to hear all the pops and creaks in your room, the hall, and Margie's and your mother's room.[13]

In his diary entry dated May 27, 1945, the President wrote:

My daughter and her two pals, Jane Lingo and Mrs. Wright— both lovely kids—are sleeping in Lincoln's bed tonight. If I were not afraid it would scare them too badly, I'd have Lincoln appear. The maids and butlers swear he has appeared on several occasions. It is said that even Mrs. Coolidge saw him.[14]

Truman had another encounter that he couldn't explain on September 7, 1946. Here's what he had to say to his wife about it:

[The] night before last I went to bed at nine o'clock after shutting all my doors. At four o'clock I was awakened by three distinct knocks on my bedroom door. I jumped up and put on my bathrobe, opened the door and no one there. Went out and looked up and down the hall, looked into your room and Margie's. Still no one. Went back to bed after locking the doors and there were footsteps in your room whose door I'd left open. Jumped up and looked and no one there! Damn place is haunted sure as shootin'. Secret Service said not even a watchman was up here at that hour. You and Margie had better come back and protect me before some of these ghosts carry me off. . . .[15]

In spite of his time away from the Executive Mansion, Truman viewed the White House as his personal prison. The pressures of running the United States during World War II and rebuilding the economy afterward were great, and he felt disconnected from the rest of the country. Although he felt isolated, clearly he wasn't completely alone—he certainly felt that some ghostly past Presidents were there with him. Maybe the ghosts of the White House were there to warn President Truman that the Executive Residence was in dire need of repair. After all, we have found through other ghost investigations that altering a building will often stir up the ghosts of the past. Whatever the case, considering the way President Truman documented his ghost sightings and how often he discussed the topic, he may well have been America's first ghost-hunting President.

Chief Usher Gary J. Walters worked at the White House from 1970 to 2007. Mr. Walters had his own brush with the unexplained while walking through the building.

Life in the White House Today

Ghosts and spirits are elusive. When and where they will show up is not predictable, and the amount of time a ghost is around may be as short as a few seconds. If you go to the White House for a tour or official visit, there is a chance that you may catch a glimpse of something unexplained. But if you work or live in the building, your chances of seeing something are much higher.

As part of our investigation, we'll need to hear from a White House insider—someone who knows the building well and who knows everything that occurs under its roof. Fortunately, we have just the person. His name is Gary J. Walters. He worked in the White House for almost 37 years. As the White House Chief Usher, Mr. Walters ran the Executive Mansion for the President.

He and his staff were in charge of making sure that every part of the President's and the First Family's lives were comfortable, that the White House tours and museum ran smoothly, and that the many official ceremonies that took place under the White House's roof and on the grounds ran perfectly.

Mr. Walters began working at the White House in 1970, when he served as a Secret Service officer for President Richard Nixon. That means he has personally known and served seven Presidents and their families. He's one of only eight people to have held the position of chief usher. It was nice of him to take time out of his busy schedule to speak to us about this building. Let's ask him some questions.

Visitors to Washington, DC, view the White House.

When did you first hear that the White House may be haunted?

There have been stories that go back all the way to when Mrs. Lincoln held séances. I don't think there's ever been an old house that hasn't had [ghost] stories attached to it.

When President Adams moved into the house, the house was not complete. There were stories that even went around then.

So is the White House haunted?

All of the Presidents and the First Ladies that I've had the pleasure of serving have referred in one way or another to a presence—a feeling of the people preceding them—the fact that they've walked down the same halls, stood in the same rooms, sat on the same furniture, and dealt with the same kinds of activities from time to time. They all have referred to the feeling of the presence of past Presidents and First Ladies who have occupied the house. As to whether any of them would absolutely say they saw a ghost or not, that's entirely different.

Has your staff reported seeing any ghosts here?

Yes, some of them do from time to time. . . . The staff doesn't say a lot, even amongst themselves, because we have a culture that's been established here through the years of privacy of the First Family. One of the operations gentlemen here said he walked into a room and saw a rocking chair move in the Lincoln Bedroom. He swears that he saw President Lincoln.

What is the most common ghost sighting here?

The name that comes up all of the time is President Lincoln. When people talk about the presidency, Lincoln is one of the first people that we think of, along with George Washington. I think that's the name that comes up because there are so many things here that are associated with Lincoln. There are so many tragedies that occurred with Lincoln and his family, and there are also the glorious things that he did.

Have you had any unexplainable experiences here in the White House?

It must've been in the late seventies or early eighties. I was standing near the stairway by the East Room in the hallway leading to the North Portico. I was there with two police officers. We were standing there talking, and each of us felt a cold rush of air go past us, and the doors that would stand open twenty-four hours a day closed behind this rush of air. I thought someone had opened a door somewhere else and created a vacuum that closed these doors, but we went and looked and nobody had opened any doors. It was very odd because, like I said, those doors stand open all the time. I just have no explanation for it. I didn't see anything, but there was a cold rush of air that passed by us.

Do you believe in ghosts?

I don't have any reason to believe, and I don't have any reason not to believe. I've never seen a ghost and never talked to a ghost.

You can't work here at the White House and not have a sense of history. You walk through the second floors and the private quarters late at night when you're turning out the lights. I don't find it an eerie feeling—I find it a wonderfully comforting feeling that this house has been occupied by so many great and glorious people.

As we conclude our ghost investigation, take one last look around the very hallway that every President since John Adams has walked through. The Presidents, members of their families, and people who have worked in this incredible building over the years have left their mark here in so many ways. Some of these people may even still be checking up on the old mansion—watching from a place just beyond where we can see. Their ghosts are here and will be for as long as the White House stands.

White House
Investigation Conclusion

A last view of the White House.

As we walk out the front door of the White House, under the North Portico, and onto the marble staircase facing Pennsylvania Avenue, we can step back into the present day. So much history and so many ghosts have passed through these walls. Be sure to turn around and take a good look at this place. Look at the windows that so many Presidents have gazed out of and notice the burn marks under the window to the right of the main door— remember what happened here? History remembers, and so do the ghosts.

There are certain criteria that we ghost investigators use to determine if a place is haunted or not. Let's run through a quick checklist:

- ✓ Have there been any deaths or tragedies at this location? *Yes*.
- ✓ Is there a history of ghost sightings here? *Yes*.
- ✓ Have the ghosts been seen or heard by more than one person? *Yes*.
- ✓ Have the ghosts been documented by witnesses in letters, diaries, or interviews? *Yes*.

Conclusion: The White House is haunted, "sure as shootin'," as President Truman said.

Before we leave, let's take one more look at what we've seen here:

Ghosts

DAVID BURNS: Once owned the land where the White House sits. His ghost has been heard in the Yellow Oval Room and on the second floor near the main staircase. ABIGAIL ADAMS: First Lady to John Adams, second President of the United States. Her ghost has been seen hanging laundry in the East Room. BRITISH REDCOAT SOLDIER: From the War of 1812. He has been seen holding his torch or lantern on the front lawn near the North Portico. ANDREW JACKSON: Seventh President of the United States. His ghost has been heard cursing in the Rose Guest Room and laughing in the Red Room.

WILLIAM HENRY HARRISON: Ninth President of the United States. He was seen and heard rummaging through the attic of the White House. WILLIE LINCOLN: Son of Abraham Lincoln, sixteenth President of the United States. He was seen by his mother, Mary Todd Lincoln, in a bedroom on the upper floor and has been experienced in other parts of the building by various staff members. THOMAS JEFFERSON: Third President of the United States. His ghost was sensed by Mary Todd Lincoln in the Yellow Oval Room. JOHN TYLER: Tenth President of the United States. Mary Todd Lincoln claimed to see him proposing to Julia Gardiner in the Yellow Oval Room just a few months after the President had died. ABRAHAM LINCOLN: Sixteenth President of the United States. The most prominent ghost in the White House, he has been seen in the Yellow Oval Room, in the Lincoln Bedroom, and in the hallway outside of the Lincoln Bedroom. DOLLEY MADISON: First Lady to James Madison, fourth President of the United States. She has been seen by the Rose Garden outside of the White House.

Although we've heard about and documented some incredible supernatural experiences, our ghost investigation doesn't end here. We'll need to check with future Presidents and First Ladies, as well as with the White House staff of tomorrow, to find out about their ghost encounters. History is still being written at the White House, and the spirits of the past are watching it all happen.

Acknowledgments

"I'm writing about the ghosts who haunt the White House," I told the many government officials, researchers, and docents I spoke to while researching and writing this book. Some didn't want to hear any more after that, but many others were intrigued at the notion of exploring the White House's history through the many ghosts that have been reported by dozens of very credible witnesses (including more than one United States President) throughout the decades. Thank you to those who gave this idea a chance and were invaluable in the gathering of history and legends.

I'd also like to thank my wife, Megan, for her unending support and critical eye, my dad for going with me to Washington, DC, (and paying for dinner), and the people who have helped along the way, including: Brooke Dworkin, Kathy Green, and Colin Quirk.

The following people and organizations were instrumental in the research of *Who's Haunting the White House?* Thank you very much to: White House Chief Usher Gary Walters, Congressman Richard E. Neal's office, Congressman Daniel Lipinski's office, David Clark at The Harry S. Truman Library & Museum, Barbara Constable at the Lyndon B. Johnson Library, the public library of Bellingham, Massachusetts, and the United States Secret Service for knowing every detail regarding the history of the building, and for keeping the White House ghosts secure.

References

1. http://www.masshist.org/digitaladams/aea/cfm/doc.cfm?id=L18001102ja

2. http://moderntimes.vcdh.virginia.edu/madison/exhibit/washington/letters/082314.html

3. http://www.mrlincolnswhitehouse.org/inside.asp?ID=18&subjectID=2

4. http://www.mrlincolnswhitehouse.org/content_inside.asp?ID=18&subjectID=2

5. *Taft and Roosevelt: The Intimate Letters of Archie Butt, Military Aide, Archibald Butt,* http://www.whitehousehistory.org/06/subs/06_c.html

6. In the July 1865 issue of *Harper's New Monthly Magazine* (at pages 224–225), Brooks retold the story using the president's own words: www.click2history.com/abraham_lincoln/abraham_lincoln_ch3.htm.

7. Ward Hill Lamon, *Recollections of Abraham Lincoln,* p. 115-118, http://www.mrlincolnswhitehouse.org/inside.asp?ID=627&subjectID=3

8. http://www.cnn.com/ALLPOLITICS/1997/02/12/lincoln.morton/

9. Betty Boyd Caroli. *Inside the White House.* New York: Canopy Books, 1992, p. 39.

10. http://www.whitehouse.gov/ghosts/

11. December 27, 1968 The View From the White House with Mrs. Lyndon B. Johnson, 1/26/2005 email from Johnson Library.

12. http://www.whitehouse.gov/ghosts/

13. The Truman Library. Family, Business & Personal Affairs Papers, Family Correspondence File, Bess Wallace Truman, 1921-1959, June 30, 1947, Box 14.

14. The Truman Library, President's Secretary's Files, Longhand Notes Files, Longhand Notes-Presidential, May 27, 1945, Box 281.

15. The Truman Library, Family, Business & Personal Affairs Papers, Family Correspondence File, Correspondence, Bess Wallace Truman, 1921-1959, September 7, 1946, Box 15.

Bibliography

Belanger, Jeff. *Communicating with the Dead: Reach beyond the Grave* (Franklin Lakes, NJ: New Page Books, 2005).

Belanger, Jeff. *The World's Most Haunted Places: From the Secret Files of Ghostvillage.com* (Franklin Lakes, NJ: New Page Books, 2004).

Caroli, Betty Boyd. *Inside the White House* (New York: Canopy Books, 1992).

Clinton, Hillary Rodham. *An Invitation to the White House: At Home with History* (New York: Simon & Schuster, 2000).

Ferrell, Robert H., ed. *Dear Bess: The Letters from Harry to Bess Truman 1910-1959* (New York: W.W. Norton & Company, 1983).

Ferrell, Robert H., ed. *Off the Record: The Private Papers of Harry S. Truman* (New York: Harper & Row, 1980).

Hakim, Joy. *A History of Us: From Colonies to Country: 1710-1791* (New York: Oxford University Press, 1999).

Holzer, Hans. *White House Ghosts* (New York: Leisure Books, 1976).

Martin, Joel and William J. Birnes. *The Haunting of the President: A Paranormal History of the U.S. Presidency* (New York: Signet, 2003).

McCullough, David. *Truman* (New York: Simon & Schuster, 1992).

Parks, Lillian Rogers. *My Thirty Years Backstairs at the White House* (New York: Fleet Publishing Corporation, 1961).

Whitcomb, John, and Claire Whitcomb. *Real Life at the White House: 200 Years of Daily Life at America's Most Famous Residence* (New York: Routledge, 2000).

White House Historical Association, The. *The White House* (Washington, D.C.: The White House Historical Association, 1964).

http://WhiteHouse.gov "Ghosts of the White House" 4 Dec. 2006. http://www.whitehouse.gov/ghosts/.

http://WhiteHouseHistory.org "The White House Time Machine" 20 Jan. 2006 http://www.whitehousehistory.org/05/subs_machine/index.html>.

Photo Credits

Index

For my daughter, Sophie,
who will never be afraid of ghosts.

BOO!